JANE ASHER

Decorated Cakes

Photography by Philip Wilkins

WEIDENFELD & NICOLSON

Jane Asher

Jane Asher is an actress, writer and businesswoman. She has appeared in plays, films, radio and television productions, and her first novel, *The Longing*, was published in 1996. She runs her own business, Jane Asher Party Cakes Shop and Tea Room in Chelsea, designs cakes for Sainsbury's and is a consultant to McVities Biscuits, Cakes and Frozen Desserts.

Her first book, *Jane Asher's Party Cakes*, was published in 1982. Since then she has written more than a dozen books on cakes, parties, cooking for children and entertaining, including *Easy Entertaining, Children's Parties* and *Calendar of Cakes*.

Contents

THE BASICS

Dost thou think,
because thou art virtuous,
there shall be no more
cakes and ale?

SIR TOBY BELCH (TWELFTH NIGHT)
WILLIAM SHAKESPEARE

Introduction

I have been making and designing decorated cakes for many years now, and I never tire of them. When I first taught myself icing techniques as a teenager, my cakes all tended to look rather formal and serious, and it was only after someone said to me that they looked so professional that they 'could have come from a bakery' that I resolved from then on to make my designs original, unusual and relevant to the person for whom they were made. The cakes in this book are some of my favourites from the many thousands I have created for customers in my shop since those early days, and I think you'll find you will be able to make them at home if you follow the instructions carefully.

All through the year there are special occasions to celebrate, and a cake is one of the best ways of marking them. The decorated cake is a very important part of anniversaries of all kinds, and has been a symbolic centrepiece at celebrations since Elizabethan times. When you make someone a cake you are not only showing that you appreciate them, but you are giving them some of your skill, time and effort.

It would have been impossible for me to design and recreate all the cakes in this book without my talented and enthusiastic team at Jane Asher Party Cakes. I would particularly like to thank Ruth Clark, Sue Spiller, Mark Knight, Wendy Mills and Isobel Rae for their hard work, skill and support.

The selection I have given covers every type of occasion, from children's parties to weddings, and I'm sure you'll be able to find something just right for you. I do hope you enjoy making them as much as I have enjoyed designing them.

CHOCOLATE TRUFFLE CAKE

20 cm/8 inch round chocolate
    sponge (page 37)
5 tablespoons Grand Marnier
    (optional)
1–2 tablespoons cocoa powder
50 g/2 oz chocolate strands

Ganache
300 ml/10 fl oz double cream
325 g/12 oz plain chocolate,
    chopped
85 g/3 oz butter, softened

To decorate
chocolate curls
fresh fruit

First make the ganache: put the cream in a saucepan, bring to the boil, then stir in the chocolate until smooth. Remove 2 tablespoons of the mixture and set aside. Leave the mixture to cool, whisking occasionally to prevent a skin from forming. When cool, whisk thoroughly and beat in the softened butter.

Slice the sponge into three layers. Sprinkle the bottom layer with 2 tablespoons of the Grand Marnier, if using, and spread with one-third of the ganache, then put the second layer on top. Sprinkle with Grand Marnier and spread with ganache as before, then add the third layer of sponge. Sprinkle with the remaining Grand Marnier, then spread the remaining ganache all over the cake.

Place a tiny amount of ganache into a piping bag and pipe an abstract design on top of the cake. Dust with cocoa powder. Coat the sides in chocolate strands and place in the refrigerator to set for 10–15 minutes.

Put the reserved chocolate cream in a piping bag and fill in the abstract design. Decorate the cake with chocolate curls and fruit.

White chocolate wedding cake

30 cm/12 inch, 22 cm/9 inch
and 15 cm/6 inch round
chocolate sponges (page 37)
3 kg/6 lb buttercream (page 38:
make 10 times the amount)
2.2 kg/5 lb ready-to-roll icing
225 g/8 oz royal icing (page 38)
1.5 kg/3 lb white chocolate drops

To decorate
fresh, silk or dried flowers
and leaves

Equipment
45 cm/18 inch round cake
board/drum
22 cm/9 inch round thin
(4 mm) board
15 cm/6 inch round thin
(4 mm) board
8 plastic dowels
palette knife
metal scraper

Slice each of the sponge cakes into three layers. Sandwich the layers with buttercream and spread a thin layer over the top and sides. Place the large sponge on the 45 cm/ 18 inch cake board, the 22 cm/9 inch sponge on the 22 cm/9 inch card and the small sponge on the 15 cm/ 6 inch card.

Divide the ready-to-roll icing into three and roll out thinly to cover all three cakes separately (page 39).

Place four plastic dowels into each of the two larger cakes, to support the boards on top. Remove the dowels, trim to be flush with the top of the cake and reinsert. Place the 22 cm/9 inch cake on top of the 30 cm/ 12 inch one and the 15 cm/6 inch cake on top of the 22 cm/9 inch one, making sure they are all in the centre. Secure using a little royal icing.

Melt the white chocolate drops in a bowl over a saucepan of hot water. Using a palette knife, spread the chocolate, in small amounts at a time, evenly and thinly on to a clean, dry, smooth surface (a marble slab is ideal). Leave to set. Using a metal scraper, holding it at an angle, push along the top of the chocolate to form curls. Store in the refrigerator. If there is any chocolate left on the surface, scrape it off and melt it down again.

Place the chocolate curls all around the sides of the cakes, securing with royal icing. Sprinkle any broken bits on the tops of the cakes. Decorate with flowers or leaves of your choice.

Cat napping!

20 cm/8 inch round fruit cake
(page 37)
125 g/4 oz apricot jam, boiled
icing sugar for dusting
675 g/1½ lb marzipan
1.5 kg/3 lb ready-to-roll icing:
650 g/1 lb 6 oz pale brown,
325 g/12 oz black,
225 g/8 oz ivory,
125 g/4 oz bottle green,
50 g/2 oz white
food colours: brown, black,
cream, green, pale pink

Equipment
pastry brush
30 cm/12 inch round cake board
basketweave rolling pin
fishbone tool
fine paintbrush

Trim the cake to an oval. Brush all over with the apricot jam. Dust a work surface with icing sugar, roll out the marzipan and use to cover the cake (page 39). Place on the board and leave to dry.

Roll out a quarter of the pale brown icing and cover the top of the cake (page 39). Roll out the rest of the brown icing into a strip long enough to encircle the cake. Indent with the basketweave rolling pin, then stick around the sides of the cake, attaching with a little water; trim. Knead the trimmings together and roll out two long sausages. Twist them together and stick around the top of the cake.

Knead and roll out the ivory icing, dampen the cake board and drape the icing around the basket. Trim off any excess.

Using half of the black icing, make a teardrop shape for the cat's body and stick on top of the cake. Make a tapering sausage shape for the tail and attach to the body. Make two shorter sausage shapes for the paws and attach. Roll a large ball for the cat's head, stick in place and add two triangles for ears.

Using the white icing, add a little to the end of the cat's tail and paws, using the fishbone tool to blend and mark. Make the features for the cat's face from the white icing, then colour the trimmings pink and make the nose and inner ears. Paint the eyes.

Roll out the green icing and mark the quilted pattern with the fishbone tool. Trim to a rectangle and stick to the top of the cake with a little water.

EXOTIC FRUITS

20 cm/8 inch round fruit cake
(page 37)
125 g/4 oz apricot jam, boiled
icing sugar for dusting
1.2 kg/2 lb 12 oz marzipan
1.1 kg/2½ lb ready-to-roll icing:
450 g/1 lb yellow,
450 g/1 lb pale brown,
225 g/8 oz white
food colours: yellow, brown,
tangerine, peach, cream,
green, red, black
450 g/1 lb pastillage (page 38),
coloured green
1 tablespoon royal icing
(page 38)
125 g/4 oz caster sugar

Equipment
pastry brush
40 x 36 cm/16 x 14 inch
cake board
fishbone tool
fine paintbrush

Trim the cake to an oval and use the trimmings to build up the height, sticking to the base cake with apricot jam. Brush all over with the jam. Dust a work surface with icing sugar, roll out 900 g/2 lb of the marzipan and use to cover the cake (page 39). Place on the board and leave to dry.

Roll out a quarter of the yellow icing and cut out lots of 2.5 cm/1 inch squares. Using a little water, stick them all over the cake in a diagonal pattern. Roll out the rest of the yellow icing and completely cover the pineapple, again sticking with a little water. Use your little finger to ease the icing into the gaps between the squares of icing underneath. Use the fishbone tool to score the pattern on the pineapple. Using tangerine, peach, cream, brown and green food colours, paint the pineapple.

Dampen the cake board with water. Knead and roll out the pale brown icing and cover the board. Knead the trimmings together and mould the root leaves; attach to the base of the fruit with a little water. Make a teardrop of pale brown for each of the individual segments of the fruit and use the fishbone tool to blend and score them.

Knead and roll out the pastillage and cut out lots of leaves. Leave to dry overnight, curved over a large rolling pin.

Use trimmings of pastillage to make a long cone, stick on to the board at the top of the fruit and stick the leaves into it, using a little royal icing.

Colour the caster sugar with cream food colour and sprinkle over the board. Model the other fruits, using the remaining marzipan. The papaya pips are made from tiny balls of black icing; other details are painted on.

VALENTINE'S BED

20 cm/8 inch square chocolate
    sponge (page 37)
600 g/1¼ lb buttercream (page
    38: make twice the amount)
2.2 kg/5 lb ready-to-roll icing:
    1.8 kg/4 lb white,
    400 g/14 oz red,
    25 g/1 oz brown,
    25 g/1 oz flesh
food colours: red, brown,
    paprika/flesh
150 g/5 oz pastillage (page 38)
50 g/2 oz royal icing (page 38),
    coloured red

Equipment

36 x 30 cm/14 x 12 inch
    cake board
straight frill cutter
pastry wheel
piping nozzle (no.1)

Trim the cake to a 20 x 15 cm/ 8 x 6 inch rectangle, then slice into two layers. Sandwich the layers with buttercream and spread a thin layer over the top and sides of the cake. Place on the cake board. Roll out half the white icing and cover the cake (page 39). Roll out the pastillage and cut out a headboard shape about 15 cm/6 inches square. Leave to dry overnight, then paint brown.

Roll out the red icing and stick to the board with a little water. Roll out some more of the white icing and cut several frills to form the valance; attach to the cake with a little water. Knead the trimmings together and model the pillows and bases of the bodies. Attach to the cake with water. Roll out the brown icing, score it with the back of a knife to make the hair, then stick to the pillow. Model the feet from the flesh-coloured icing; attach to the cake.

Roll out the remaining white icing. Mark the quilting with a pastry wheel, trim to a rectangle and drape over the bed. Using the red royal icing, pipe the hearts over the quilt. Finally, stick on the headboard.

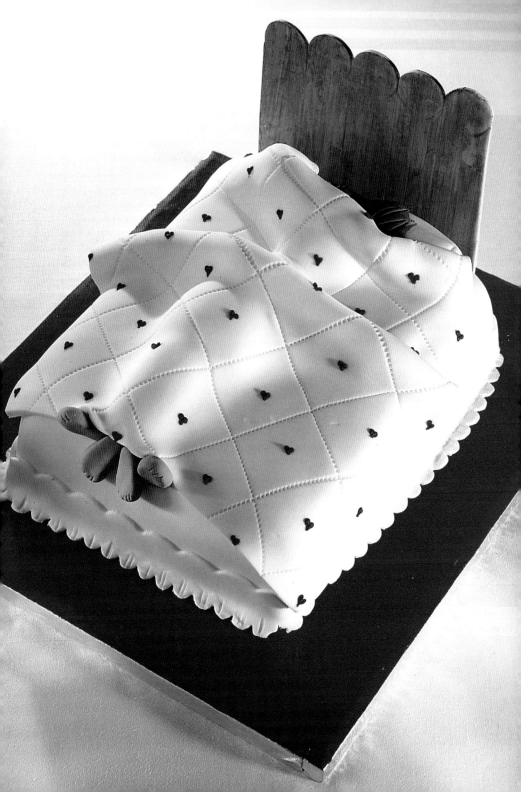

CHRISTENING CAKE

20 cm/8 inch round fruit cake
(page 37)
125 g/4 oz apricot jam, boiled
icing sugar for dusting
900 g/2 lb marzipan
1.1 kg/2 ½ lb ready-to-roll icing:
    850 g/1 lb 14 oz white,
    225 g/8 oz yellow,
    50 g/2 oz brown
food colours: yellow, brown,
    pink, black
125 g/4 oz royal icing (page 38)

Equipment
pastry brush
30 cm/12 inch round cake board
fine paintbrush
piping nozzles (no.1 and no.3)

Brush the cake with the apricot jam. Dust a work surface with icing sugar, roll out the marzipan and use to cover the cake (page 39). Place on the board and leave to dry.

Roll out the white icing and cover the cake (page 39). Knead the trimmings together and roll out a long strip of icing to cover the board, sticking with a little water.

Using a no.3 piping nozzle, pipe a royal icing snail's trail around the base of the cake.

Roll out half the yellow icing and cut 6 equal strips about 15 cm/6 inches long and 5 mm/¼ inch wide. Twist each strip, and stick to the sides of the cake with a little water. Reroll the trimmings and more yellow icing to make the bows and tails: the bows are made from strips of icing, the ends folded into the centre and a small piece of icing wrapped around the join. Stick to the top of each swag.

Model the rabbit, teddy, building blocks and balls from the remaining icing, and paint on the details. Stick on to the cake with water or a little royal icing.

Colour the remaining royal icing pale yellow. Using the no.1 piping nozzle, write the name and pipe a simple pattern around the board.

PORSCHE 911

25 cm/10 inch square fruit cake
(page 37)
125 g/4 oz apricot jam, boiled
icing sugar for dusting
1.5 kg/3 lb marzipan
2 kg/4½ lb ready-to-roll icing:
   1.5 kg/3 lb dark green,
   450 g/1 lb white,
   225 g/8 oz black
food colours: green, black,
   silver*, orange, yellow, red

Equipment
pastry brush
40 x 36 cm/16 x 14 inch
   cake board
fishbone tool
4 cm/1½ inch round cutter
fine paintbrush

* Although the silver colour is
non-toxic, it is not suitable for ·
consumption and should be
removed before eating.

Cut the cake into two 25 x 12 cm/10 x 5 inch cakes. Cut a 5 cm/2 inch slice off one of the cakes, and stick this piece to the end of the other half of the cake with apricot jam. Brush the top with apricot jam and place the remaining 20 x 12 cm/8 x 5 inch piece on top. Place on the board. Dust a work surface with icing sugar, roll out the marzipan and use to cover the cake (page 39). Knead the trimmings together and use to build up the wings and wheel arches, attaching them with a little water. Leave to dry.

Roll a small amount of black icing into a long strip, approximately 2.5 cm/1 inch wide. Stick all around the bottom of the car. Brush the whole cake with water. Roll out the green icing, lay over the car and smooth into place. Trim off the icing where it reaches the black strip and trim around the wheel arches. Using the fishbone tool, mark the windows, doors and bonnet. Using a sharp knife, carefully remove the green icing in the windows and replace with thinly rolled black icing. Cut out four wheels of black icing. Paint the wire wheels or hub caps with silver food colour and leave to dry.

Using the green icing trimmings, mould the front and back bumpers and wing mirrors; attach with a little water. Roll out a little white icing and cut out the headlights, indicators and registration plates; paint appropriately and stick to the car. Using black icing, mould the window trims, door handles and windscreen wipers and stick to the car.

Knead and roll out the remaining white icing, dampen the cake board and cover with the icing. If you like, crimp the edges of the iced board. Finally, stick the wheels in place.

SWEET CASCADE

20 cm/8 inch round chocolate
   sponge (page 37)
chocolate buttercream (page 38)
about 200 g/7 oz sweets
about 200 g/7 oz soft fruits

Stock syrup
50 g/2 oz sugar
1 lemon, sliced
1–2 tablespoons rum
   or amaretto

Boiled chocolate icing
275 g/10 oz caster sugar
125 g/4 oz plain chocolate,
   chopped
50 g/2 oz cocoa powder, sifted

Equipment
pastry brush
25 cm/10 inch round cake board
sugar thermometer

First make the stock syrup: put the sugar and lemon in a small saucepan with 150 ml/5 fl oz water. Bring to the boil, boil for 5 minutes, then leave to cool. Add the rum or amaretto, if using.

Slice the sponge into three layers and brush all three layers with the syrup. Place the bottom layer on the cake board. Spread with buttercream, add the second layer, spread with buttercream, then add the top layer. Spread a thin layer of buttercream over the top and sides of the cake and place in the refrigerator to set.

Make the chocolate icing: put the sugar, chocolate and cocoa into a heavy-bottomed saucepan. Add 8 tablespoons water and stir thoroughly with a wooden spoon. Stirring all the time, bring to the boil. Place a sugar thermometer in the mixture and cook until it reaches 108°C/220°F or the long thread stage, brushing the edge of the saucepan frequently with water to prevent the mixture from crystallizing. Pour into a heatproof bowl and beat well until thick and glossy. To cool quickly, pour half on to a clean, dry work surface and work with a palette knife, then return to the bowl.

Place the cake on a wire rack, pour over the cooled chocolate icing and spread with a palette knife. Leave to set.

Place the cake back on the board and decorate: stick on the sweets and fruits with a little of the chocolate icing and pipe around the base.

BASKET OF WINE

25 cm/10 inch square fruit cake
 (page 37)
125 g/4 oz apricot jam, boiled
icing sugar for dusting
900 g/2 lb marzipan
1.3 kg/2 lb 12 oz ready-to-roll
 icing: 1.1 kg/2½ lb cream,
 125 g/4 oz black,
 25 g/1 oz red
food colours: cream, black,
 red, brown
225 g/8 oz pastillage (page 38)
450 g/1 lb royal icing
 (page 38)

Equipment
pastry brush
40 x 25 cm/16 x 10 inch
 cake board
piping nozzles (basketweave
 and no.4)
fine paintbrush

Cut the cake into two 25 x 12 cm/10 x 5 inch cakes. Slice one of the cakes in half horizontally. Stick half on top of the 25 x 12 cm/10 x 5 inch cake with apricot jam. Trim the other half to a domed bottle shape and stick on top of the rectangular cake. Brush all over with apricot jam. Dust a work surface with icing sugar, roll out the marzipan and use to cover the cake (page 39). Place on the board and leave to dry.

Roll out 800 g/1¾ lb of the cream icing and cover the cake (page 39). Cut the icing off the bottle and replace with thinly rolled black icing. Form the neck of the bottle from the red icing – it should overhang the edge of the cake. Roll out the pastillage into two long sausages and form the handles for the basket. Leave to dry for at least 24 hours.

Roll out a little cream icing, cut out a rectangle for the label and stick to the bottle. Paint on a suitable design. Colour the royal icing pale brown and, using the piping nozzles, pipe the basketweave around the cake.

Roll out some more cream icing and form the folds of the napkin around the bottle and on the board, sticking with a little water. Finally, paint and stick on the handle of the basket, supporting it with cocktail sticks until it dries.

Mermaid

20 cm/8 inch round fruit cake
(page 37)
125 g/4 oz apricot jam, boiled
icing sugar for dusting
900 g/2 lb marzipan
225 g/8 oz pastillage (page 38):
125 g/4 oz white,
50 g/2 oz green,
50 g/2 oz dark paprika
1.6 kg/3½ lb ready-to-roll icing:
675 g /1½ lb grey,
325 g/12 oz cream,
175 g/6 oz paprika/flesh,
125 g/4 oz purple,
50 g/2 oz black,
50 g/2 oz white
food colours: spruce green,
paprika, black, cream,
grape violet, ice blue, white,
red, yellow, pink
dusting powder: black,
honey pearl
50 g/2 oz royal icing (page 38)

Equipment
pastry brush
36 cm/14 inch round cake board
24-gauge floristry wire
ball tool
fine paintbrush
piping nozzle (no.3)

Cut the cake into a rock shape, using the trimmings to build up height. Brush with jam, cover with marzipan (page 39) and leave to dry. Roll out the green pastillage thinly and cut out lots of seaweed. Leave to dry overnight on crumpled foil. Roll out 25 g/1 oz of white pastillage and cut out two fish. Skewer on to wires and leave to dry overnight before painting.

Roll out the grey icing and cover the cake (page 39). Use the trimmings to make the rock ledges; attach to the cake. Shade the rock with black dusting powder. Roll out the cream icing and cover the board (page 39). Using the ball tool, indent the ripples around the rock.

For the oyster, use the black icing to make a ball. Make the shell using 25 g/1 oz of white pastillage; stick to the ball. Pipe some royal icing over the shell and smooth out slightly with a damp brush. When dry, paint with diluted honey pearl powder. Make the eyes from a little white icing, stick on and paint the centres black.

For the mermaid, form the body and tail from 150 g/ 5 oz of the flesh-coloured icing. Score scales on the tail, then paint blue and green. Using the white icing, model the tail fins, then paint with honey pearl powder and ice blue. Model the head, neck and arms and attach to the body with water. Paint on the face. Colour a pinch of icing green and make the bikini top; attach to the body. Using the paprika pastillage, model the hair and attach.

Make the octopus from the purple icing, mark with the tip of the piping nozzle and stick to the cake. Make the coral from the remaining pastillage, thin the edges and dot with cocktail sticks; attach to the rock. Push the seaweed gently into the icing and position the fish.

CHRISTMAS CAKE

20 cm/8 inch round fruit cake
(page 37)
125 g/4 oz apricot jam, boiled
icing sugar for dusting
900 g/2 lb marzipan
1.1 kg/2½ lb ready-to-roll icing
1 tablespoon royal icing
(page 38)
food colours: gold*, red, green
85 g/3 oz petal paste (page 38):
25 g/1 oz red,
25 g/1 oz green,
25 g/1 oz white

Equipment
pastry brush
cake smoother
30 cm/12 inch round cake board
garrett frill cutter
piping nozzle (no.1)
poinsettia cutter
ball tool
grooved petal board
holly cutter
26-gauge floristry wire
ivy cutter
floristry tape

* Although the gold colour is
non-toxic, it is not suitable for
consumption and should be
removed before eating.

Brush the cake with the apricot jam. Dust a work surface with icing sugar, roll out the marzipan and use to cover the cake (page 39). Place on the board and leave to dry.

Roll out the icing and cover the cake (page 39). Knead the trimmings together and roll out a long strip of icing to cover the board, sticking with a little water. Dust the work surface generously with icing sugar to prevent sticking, roll out some white icing thinly and cut out six frills. Ruffle the edges of each one with a cocktail stick and attach to the sides of the cake with a little water. Add a second layer of frills. Using the no.1 piping nozzle and a little royal icing, pipe a holly pattern around the top of the frills. Leave to dry, then paint gold.

Roll out the red petal paste and cut out five large poinsettia petals. Indent the veins and thin the edge slightly with the ball tool. Leave to dry in a foil cup. Make five smaller red petals, and five large green petals. Add a pinch of white petal paste to a pinch of green, roll out and cut the calyx. When all the petals are dry, stick together with a little red royal icing.

Using the grooved petal board, roll out the green petal paste very thinly, cut out the holly and insert the floristry wire. Thin the edges slightly and leave to dry. Using the white petal paste, repeat the process to make the ivy. When dry, paint the ivy gold. The holly berries are made from small balls of red petal paste, on wires.

To assemble, tape the leaves together in small sprigs. Make a small mound of icing on top of the cake and push the leaves into it, sticking the poinsettia in the centre. Using the no.1 piping nozzle, write the message.

TRADITIONAL WEDDING CAKE

15 cm/6 inch and 22 cm/9 inch
round fruit cakes (page 37)
22 cm/9 inch and 30 cm/
12 inch hexagonal fruit cakes
(page 37)
800 g/1¾ lb petal paste
(page 38)
white sugartex
food colours: gold*, cream,
Christmas green or
spruce green
dusting powders: apple green,
moss green, brown
450 g/1 lb apricot jam, boiled
icing sugar for dusting
4.2 kg/9½ lb marzipan
4.6 kg//10½ lb ivory ready-to-roll
icing
1 tablespoon royal icing
(page 38)

* Although the gold colour is
non-toxic, it is not suitable for
consumption and should be
removed before eating.

First make the flowers. For the arum lilies: tape together three 24-gauge wires; repeat three more times. Cut each in half and hook the end of each. Roll tapering sausages of petal paste, about 8 cm/3 inches long and 5 mm/¼ inch wide at the base. Dip the hooked end of the taped wire in water and insert halfway into the icing: this forms the 'tongue' of the lily. Leave overnight to dry in a curved shape.

The next day, dampen with a little water and coat in sugartex. When dry, paint with gold food colour and leave to dry for 1 hour. Roll out some white petal paste very thinly. Cut a large teardrop shape, about 10 cm/4 inches long. Dampen the base with a little water and wrap around the base of the 'tongue'. Place in the foam, with the heads of the flowers hanging downwards, and leave to dry for at least 6 hours.

For the roses: as for the arum lilies, tape 24-gauge wires together in bunches of three, cut them in half and hook the ends. You will need 15–20 of these. Using petal paste, make a cone for each rose, about 2.5–4 cm/1–1½ inches long, attach to a wire and leave to dry overnight.

Make a cardboard template for a rose petal, about 5 cm/2 inches long and 4 cm/1½ inches wide. Colour 50 g/2 oz of petal paste dark cream. Roll out very thinly and use the template to cut two petals for each rose. Gently lift up one of the petals, and cover the rest with a plastic bag to prevent them from drying out. Dust the palm of your hand with icing sugar and rest the petal in the centre. Using the ball tool, thin the outside edge of the petal. Brush the base and sides with water and wrap tightly around a cone. Repeat with another petal, with the centre of the second petal over

Equipment

floristry tape

24- and 26-gauge floristry wires

foam or oasis to support the
  flowers while drying

ball tool

grooved petal board

ivy cutter

medium paintbrush

15 cm/6 inch and 22 cm/9 inch
  round thin (4 mm) boards

28 cm/11 inch and 40 cm/
  16 inch hexagonal cake
  boards/drums

pastry brush

cake smoother

spiked pastry wheel

12 plastic dowels

piping nozzle (no.3)

4 gold cupid pillars

the join of the first. Add two petals to all the roses.
Leave to dry in foam or oasis.

Add a further 50 g/2 oz of white petal paste to the
cream paste. Roll out very thinly and cut three petals
for each rose. Take three petals at a time, thin the edges
and stick to the rose with a little water. Each petal
should overlap the previous one, and the tips should
curl outwards.

Add another 50 g/2 oz of white paste to the pale
cream, roll out and cut five petals for about three-
quarters of the roses. Thin the edges and attach to the
roses, overlapping each petal. Repeat with another layer
of five petals for 6–8 of the roses. Let these larger roses
dry hanging upside down, as they tend to droop.

For the leaves: cut the 26-gauge wires into thirds or
quarters. Set aside 125 g/4 oz of white petal paste, then
colour the rest dark green. Using the grooved petal
board, roll out some green paste thinly. Cut out ivy in
three sizes, plus some thinner leaves, 5–8 cm/2–3
inches long and 5 mm/¼ inch wide. Dip the ends of
the wires into water, then insert into the leaves. Gently
place in the palm of your hand and thin the edges using
the ball tool. You could also vein each leaf, either with a
cocktail stick or with a plastic leaf former. Make as many
leaves as you have patience for! Let the leaves dry for a
couple of hours. Using a dry brush, shade the leaves with
the dusting powders. Tape the leaves together in sprigs.

Place each cake on its board and brush with apricot
jam. Dust a work surface with icing sugar, roll out the
marzipan and cover the cakes (page 39). Leave to dry.

Roll out the icing and cover the cakes (page 39) – the boards under the two round cakes should not now be visible. Roll out a strip of icing and wrap around the boards of the two hexagonal cakes, sticking with a little water. Using the pastry wheel and a ruler as a guide, mark the two round cakes with a quilted pattern.

Push four plastic dowels into the middle of each hexagonal cake, and cut off where they reach the top of the iced cake. These will support the weight of the cake above. Gently place the round quilted cakes on top of the plain hexagonal ones, using a little royal icing to secure. Using the no.3 piping nozzle, pipe a royal icing snail's trail around the base of each cake, and pipe a dot on the converging lines of the quilted cakes.

Knead the trimmings of icing with the reserved 125 g/ 4 oz of petal paste. Roll out thinly and cut out 12 rectangles, about 4–5 cm/1½–2 inches deep and as long as each side of the hexagonal cakes. Pleat each rectangle and attach to the side of the cake with a little water. Reroll the trimmings to make the bows and tails: the bows are made from strips of icing, the ends folded into the centre and pinched together, with a small piece of icing wrapped around the join. Attach to the cake and leave to dry, then paint the drapes, bows and dots with gold colour.

Position the pillars on the cake and insert the dowel supports. Make a mound of icing for each round cake. Leave to dry for 1 hour, then push in the flowers and leaves. Start with the arum lilies, then the roses, then fill in any gaps with the foliage. Position the pillars on top of the dowel supports and fix with a little royal icing.

The Basics

Square	12 cm/5 inch	15 cm/6 inch	18 cm/7 inch	20 cm/8 inch	22 cm/9 inch	25 cm/10 inch	28 cm/11 inch
Round/hexagonal	15 cm/6 inch	18 cm/7 inch	20 cm/8 inch	22 cm/9 inch	25 cm/10 inch	28 cm/11 inch	30 cm/12 inch
RICH FRUIT CAKE							
Mixed dried fruit	425 g/15 oz	650 g/1 lb 7 oz	800 g/1 lb 14 oz	1 kg/2 lb 6 oz	1.5 kg/3 lb 5 oz	1.8 kg/4 lb 2 oz	2.2 kg/5 lb 2 oz
Glacé cherries	50 g/2 oz	85 g/3 oz	150 g/5 oz	175 g/6 oz	250 g/9 oz	275 g/10 oz	325 g/12 oz
Mixed peel	25 g/1 oz	50 g/2 oz	85 g/3 oz	125 g/4 oz	150 g/5 oz	200 g/7 oz	250 g/9 oz
Flaked almonds (optional)	25 g/1 oz	50 g/2 oz	85 g/3 oz	125 g/4 oz	150 g/5 oz	200 g/7 oz	225 g/8 oz
Ground mixed spice (teaspoons)	½	1	1½	2	2½	3	5
Lemon zest (grated)	½	½	1	1	1½	2	2½
Brandy (tablespoons)	1	1	1½	2	2½	3	5
Butter	160 g/5½ oz	175 g/6 oz	275 g/10 oz	325 g/12 oz	500 g/1 lb 2 oz	600 g/1 lb 5oz	675 g/1½ lb
Soft dark brown sugar	160 g/5½ oz	175 g/6 oz	275 g/10 oz	325 g/12 oz	500 g/1 lb 2oz	600 g/1 lb 5oz	675 g/1½ lb
Eggs (medium)	2	3	5	6	8	9	10
Plain flour	200 g/7 oz	225 g/8 oz	325 g/12 oz	400 g/14 oz	600 g/1 lb 5oz	675 g/1½ lb	800 g/1 lb 12oz
Cooking time (approx)	3¾ hours	3¾ hours	4¾ hours	5½ hours	6½ hours	7¼ hours	8½ hours
SPONGE CAKE							
Butter	50 g/2 oz	135 g/4½oz	175 g/6 oz	225 g/8 oz	325 g/12 oz	450 g/1 lb	500 g/1 lb 2 oz
Caster sugar	50 g/2 oz	135 g/4½oz	175 g/6 oz	225 g/8 oz	325 g/12 oz	450 g/1 lb	500 g/1 lb 2 oz
Eggs (medium)	1	2	3	4	6	8	9
Self-raising flour	50 g/2 oz	135 g/4½oz	175 g/6 oz	225 g/8 oz	325 g/12 oz	450 g/1 lb	500 g/1 lb 2 oz
CHOCOLATE SPONGE							
Replace these amounts of flour with cocoa powder	15 g/½ oz	20 g/¾ oz	25 g/1 oz	40 g/1½ oz	50 g/2 oz	125 g/4 oz	175 g/6 oz
Cooking time	30 minutes	40 minutes	50 minutes	1 hour	1¼ hours	1½ hours	1¾ hours

RICH FRUIT CAKE

Place the dried fruit, cherries, peel, almonds, spice and lemon zest in a large bowl. Pour over the brandy and mix well. Leave to soak overnight.

Double line the base and sides of an 8 cm/3 inch deep cake tin with greaseproof paper. Wrap the outside with double-thickness brown paper, secure with string. Place on a baking sheet lined with 3–4 thicknesses of brown paper or newspaper. Preheat the oven to 140°C/275°F/Gas Mark 1.

Cream the butter and sugar until light and fluffy. Add the eggs one at a time, beating well after each addition. Fold in the sifted flour, then the fruit mixture. Place in the prepared tin and smooth the top with the back of a wet metal spoon. Bake (see chart).

Leave the cake to cool in the tin. When cold, turn out and wrap in foil until required.

SPONGE CAKE

Double line the base and sides of an 8 cm/3 inch deep cake tin with greaseproof paper. Preheat the oven to 170°C/325°F/Gas Mark 3.

Cream the butter and sugar until light and fluffy. Add the eggs one at a time, beating well after each addition. Fold in the sifted flour, place in the prepared tin and bake (see chart).

Test by pressing the centre with your fingers – it will spring back and feel firm when cooked. Turn out on to a wire rack and leave until cold.

BUTTERCREAM

125 g/4 oz butter, softened
175 g/6 oz icing sugar
2 tablespoons hot water
2–3 drops of vanilla essence
  (optional)

Beat the butter in a bowl until light and fluffy. Gradually beat in the icing sugar and then the hot water and vanilla, if using.

For chocolate buttercream, melt 50 g/2 oz dark chocolate and beat in with the hot water.

ROYAL ICING

2 egg whites
2 teaspoons lemon juice
450 g/1 lb icing sugar, sifted

Using a fork, beat the egg whites in a bowl, whisk in the lemon juice, then add the icing sugar a little at a time, beating well.

PASTILLAGE

450 g/1 lb icing sugar
125 g/4 oz cornflour
2 teaspoons gum tragacanth
2 leaves of gelatine
1 teaspoon liquid glucose

Sift the icing sugar, cornflour and gum tragacanth together into a bowl. Dissolve the gelatine in 5 tablespoons water, add the glucose and then add the liquid to the dry ingredients. Beat well to form a paste, then knead until smooth. Keep in a plastic bag until required.

PETAL PASTE

450 g/1 lb icing sugar
1 teaspoon gum tragacanth
2 teaspoons powdered gelatine
5 teaspoons white fat
2 teaspoons liquid glucose
1 egg white

Sift the icing sugar and gum tragacanth into a bowl and stand it over hot water to warm it a little. Soak the gelatine in 5 teaspoons water, then place in a saucepan with the white fat and glucose. Place over a low heat until smooth, add the egg white then pour on to the icing sugar. Beat with an electric mixer for 2–3 minutes, or until it becomes elastic. (If you are beating by hand, you will need to do it for at least 5–10 minutes.) Keep in a plastic bag in the refrigerator for at least 30 minutes before use.

CUTTING AND SHAPING CAKES

Always use a sharp serrated knife. If you require height, pile up several cakes, sticking together with apricot jam or buttercream. Always start by carving off less then you think and trim until you get the correct shape. If gaps appear (very likely when using fruit cake) fill them with marzipan before covering.

COVERING A CAKE WITH MARZIPAN

Brush the top and sides of the cake with apricot jam that has been boiled. Sprinkle the work surface lightly with sifted icing sugar. Knead the marzipan into a ball and roll out to about 5 mm/¼ inch thick, large enough to cover the cake completely.

Roll the marzipan loosely around the rolling pin, place one edge of the marzipan at the far side of the cake and unroll it over the cake. Smooth the marzipan over the top and down the sides, using either your hand or a cake smoother. Trim the excess from the base of the cake using a small sharp knife. Leave to dry for at least 24 hours before icing.

COVERING A CAKE WITH ICING

Fruit cakes should first be marzipanned; sponge cakes should be spread with buttercream. Sprinkle the work surface lightly with sifted icing sugar. Knead the icing into a ball and roll out to about 5 mm/ ¼ inch thick.

Dampen the marzipan with a little water (which has been boiled and cooled). Lift the icing, supported by a rolling pin, over the cake. Using your hand or a cake smoother, smooth the icing over the top and down the sides, removing any air bubbles. Trim off the excess with a small sharp knife. Knead together the trimmings and seal in a plastic bag.

COVERING THE CAKE BOARD

For a round board, roll out a long strip of icing (use a piece of string to measure the length). Roll up, dampen the board with water and unroll the icing around the cake. Trim the edge.

For a square board, cut out four strips of icing, one for each side. Dampen the board, lay on the icing and cut each corner, from the corner of the cake to the corner of the board. Trim the edges.

To cover the complete board, dampen and cover, trim the edges and crimp if desired.

First published in 1997 by
George Weidenfeld & Nicolson
The Orion Publishing Group
Orion House
5 Upper St Martin's Lane
London WC2H 9EA

British Library Cataloguing-in-Publication data
A catalogue record for this book is available from
the British Library

ISBN 0 297 82333 7

Designed by Lucy Holmes
Edited by Maggie Ramsay
Typesetting by Tiger Typeset

JANE ASHER

Decorated Cakes